In Our Joy

IN OUR JOY
Published by Desiring God

Copyright © 2007 Desiring God
International Standard Book Number: 978-1-60402-877-5

Edited by Desiring God

TABLE OF CONTENTS

The kingdom of heaven is like a treasure hidden in a field, which a man found and covered up. Then in his joy he goes and sells all that he has and buys that field.

MATTHEW 13:44

INTRODUCTION

The title for this little book is adapted from one of Jesus' shortest parables:

> The kingdom of heaven is like a treasure hidden in
> a field, which a man found and covered up. Then in
> his joy he goes and sells all that he has and buys that
> field. (Matt. 13:44)

Fifteen minutes before his discovery in the field, the thought of selling all that he owned would have seemed unwise to this man, even excruciating. But fifteen minutes afterward he was off to do it with joy. What made the difference?

The treasure. This man suddenly found something that transformed his whole outlook on life. It restructured his priorities. It altered his goals. His values changed. The treasure revolutionized the man.

There was a cost to obtaining the treasure. Viewing it one way, it was a high cost. Imagine being his neighbor. You would have been bewildered as you watched him liquidate his assets. You might have questioned him. You might have warned him of the dangers of imperiling his family. You might have talked to other neighbors, wondering if the man was going bonkers. You would have been puzzled at his joy.

But viewing it another way, the cost was very small. The man was shrewd. Standing there in the field, he did a quick cost-benefit analysis. It didn't take much time to realize that selling all his possessions was going to make him wealthy beyond his wildest dreams. What he did might have appeared foolish at first. But in reality the benefits so far outweighed the costs that he would have been foolish not to sell everything.

That's what this little book is about—the treasure. And it's about the cost. There is a cost to obtaining the treasure. We must be realistic about it: it will cost us everything. But if we've really discovered the treasure, the most realistic conclusion is that we would be foolish not to go and in our joy sell all that we have to get it.

Jon Bloom, Executive Director
Desiring God

PART ONE

THE HARD ROAD
OF THE CHRISTIAN LIFE

*Come to me, all who labor and are heavy laden,
and I will give you rest.*

MATTHEW 11:28

*Jesus stood up and cried out, "If anyone thirsts,
let him come to me and drink."*

JOHN 7:37

*Jesus said to them, "I am the bread of life;
whoever comes to me shall not hunger."*

JOHN 6:35

You refuse to come to me that you may have life.

JOHN 5:40

*When he had said these things, he cried out
with a loud voice, "Lazarus, come out."
The man who had died came out.*

JOHN 11:43-44

CHAPTER ONE

COMING TO JESUS IS NOT EASY

W hen a person is born anew and experiences repentance, his attitude about Jesus changes. Jesus himself becomes the central focus and supreme value of life. Before the new birth happens and repentance occurs, a hundred other things seem more important and more attractive: health, family, job, friends, sports, music, food, sex, hobbies, retirement. But when God gives the radical change of new birth and repentance, Jesus himself becomes our supreme treasure.

HIS YOKE IS EASY, AND HIS BURDEN IS LIGHT

Therefore, his demand that we come to him is not burdensome. It means coming to the one who has become everything to us. Jesus did not come into the world mainly to bring a new religion or a new law. He came to offer himself for our eternal enjoyment and to do whatever he had to do—including death—to remove every obstacle to this everlasting joy in him. "These things I have spoken to you, that my joy may be in

you, and that your joy may be full" (John 15:11).
When Jesus demands that we do things—like "Come
to me"—the essence of these demands is that we
experience the life that most fully savors and spreads
his supreme worth.

As Jesus looks out over the religions of the
world—including the Judaism of his day—he sees
people who are laboring under heavy loads to earn
the favor of whatever deity they believe in. He did
not come to replace that God-appeasing load with
another one. He came to carry that load and call us to
himself for rest. "Come to me, all who labor and are
heavy laden, and I will give you rest. Take my yoke
upon you, and learn from me, for I am gentle and
lowly in heart, and you will find rest for your souls.
For my yoke is easy, and my burden is light" (Matt.
11:28-30). Make no mistake, there *is* a yoke and a
burden when we come to Jesus (there would be no
demands if this were not true), but the yoke is easy,
and the burden is light.

THERE IS A BURDEN, BUT IT'S NOT JESUS
But perhaps it's not easy and light the way we think
it is. Jesus also said, "The gate is narrow and the way

is *hard* that leads to life" (Matt. 7:14). The reason it is hard is not because Jesus is a hard taskmaster. It's hard because the world is a hard place to enjoy Jesus above all. Our own suicidal tendency to enjoy other things more must be crushed (Matt. 5:29-30). And besides our own sin, many people are angered that we do not love what they love. So Jesus warned, "Some of you they will put to death. You will be hated by all for my name's sake" (Luke 21:16-17).

But Jesus is not the burden. When we come to him, he is the burden-lifter, the soul-satisfier, and the life-giver. "Jesus stood up and cried out, 'If anyone thirsts, let him come to me and drink'" (John 7:37). Coming to Jesus means coming to drink. And the water we drink in fellowship with Jesus gives everlasting life. "Whoever drinks of the water that I will give him will never be thirsty forever. The water that I will give him will become in him a spring of water welling up to eternal life" (John 4:14). The demand that we come to Jesus is the demand to come to the fountain of life and drink.

Jesus is not satisfied to lure us into obedience with images of life-giving water. He will also draw us with promises of life-sustaining bread. "I am the bread of life; he who comes to me shall not hunger" (John 6:35). Jesus himself is the bread of heaven— the source and essence of everlasting life. He will draw us with promises of deliverance from perishing (John 3:16). The demand that we come to him is therefore like the demand of a father to his child in a burning window, "Jump to me!" Or like the demand of a rich, strong, tender, handsome husband to an unfaithful wife, "Come home!" Or like the demand of a rescue squad that finds you on the point of death, dehydrated after days in the desert, "Drink this!"

"YOU REFUSE TO COME TO ME THAT YOU MAY HAVE LIFE"

But the personal tragedy of sin and spiritual blindness is that people do not come. Jesus grieved over his people. "O Jerusalem, Jerusalem, the city that kills the prophets and stones those who are sent to it! How often would I have gathered your children together as a hen gathers her brood under her wings, and you would not!" (Matt. 23:37). "You search the Scriptures because you think that in them you have eternal life; and it is they that bear witness about me, yet you refuse to come to me that you may have life" (John 5:39-40).

Why don't people come to Jesus? At one level the answer is because they "*refuse* to come." In other words, people do not *want* to come. Some call this the choice of free will. Jesus would probably say it is the choice of a will enslaved to sin. "Truly, truly, I say to you, everyone who commits sin is a *slave* to sin" (John 8:34). Jesus would say that people do not come to him because they are enslaved to their supreme preference for other things. "The light has come into the world, and people loved the darkness rather than the light . . . everyone who does wicked things hates the light and does not come to the light" (John 3:19-20).

How then has anyone ever come, since we are all enslaved to sin and spiritually dead? Jesus' answer was that God, in his great mercy, overcomes our resistance and draws us: "No one can come to me unless the Father who sent me draws him" (John 6:44). "No one can come to me unless it is granted him by the Father" (John 6:65). God grants the gift of new birth and repentance, which opens the eyes of the spiritually blind to the truth and beauty of Jesus. When this happens, all suicidal objections fall. We are finally free. And, finally free from slavery, we come.

"LAZARUS, COME OUT!"

Jesus came into the world to gather his flock from all the world (John 11:52). He lays down his life for them and demands that they come to him. Though he weeps over those who do not come, he will not be frustrated in his design. He will succeed in gathering a people for himself. He speaks with absolute sovereignty when he says, "I have other sheep that are not of this fold. I must bring them also, and they will listen to my voice. So there will be one flock, one shepherd" (John 10:16). He *must* bring them. They *will* heed his voice. They *will* come.

When you hear the voice of Jesus saying, "Come to me," pray that God would give you eyes to see Jesus as irresistibly true and beautiful. Pray that you would hear this command the way Lazarus did when he was dead. "[Jesus] cried out with a loud voice, 'Lazarus, come out.' The man who had died came [out of his grave]" (John 11:43-44). When you come to Jesus like this, you will never cease to praise and thank him for his sovereign grace.

If anyone would come after me, let him deny himself and take up his cross and follow me. For whoever would save his life will lose it, but whoever loses his life for my sake will find it.

MATTHEW 16:24-25

Follow me, and I will make you become fishers of men.

MARK 1:17

I am the light of the world; he who follows me will not walk in darkness but will have the light of life.

JOHN 8:12

Follow me, and leave the dead to bury their own dead.

MATTHEW 8:22

If you would be perfect, go, sell what you possess and give to the poor, and you will have treasure in heaven; and come, follow me.

MATTHEW 19:21

CHAPTER TWO

FOLLOWING JESUS IS A HARD ROAD

Jesus' invitation to come to him was for the purpose of discipleship. When we come to Jesus, we come to *follow* him. This can be seen concretely in Jesus' life on earth. Jesus was fully human and fully God (John 1:1, 14). He was not God with a human veneer—like a costume. He was a real, flesh-and-blood man, a carpenter's son (Mark 6:3). So when he said to fishermen or tax collectors, "Follow me," their obedience was a concrete, physical act of putting their feet on the ground and walking behind Jesus and being part of his traveling team.

FOLLOWING JESUS WHEN HE IS NOT HERE

But Jesus knew that he would not always be on earth to have followers in this physical sense. "I am going to him who sent me. . . . I tell you the truth: it is to your advantage that I go away, for if I do not go away, the Helper will not come to you. But if I go, I will send him to you" (John 16:5, 7). Jesus was fully aware that the movement he began would continue after he had gone back to his Father in heaven. This was his plan.

Therefore, the demand that we follow him was relevant not only for his physical days on earth but for all time. He made this clear at the end of his earthly ministry. He had risen from the dead and was about to ascend to the Father. He told Peter that he would suffer martyrdom someday after Jesus was gone. Peter wondered if he was the only one and asked Jesus what would happen to his fellow apostle, John. Jesus answered, "If it is my will that he remain until I come, what is that to you? You follow me!" (John 21:22).

What this implies about "following Jesus" is that it happens after he is gone. Until Jesus comes again, he expects his disciples on earth to "follow" him. So following Jesus is not limited to physically walking around Palestine behind him. Jesus demands it of every person in every country in every age.

FOLLOWING JESUS MEANS JOINING HIM IN WHAT HE WAS SENT TO DO

When Jesus said to Peter and Andrew, who were fishermen by trade, "Follow me, and *I will make you become fishers of men*" (Mark 1:17), he was using imagery relevant to them for something that applies to everyone who follows Jesus. The demand to follow Jesus means that everyone should join him in what he came to do. And he tells us repeatedly what that was. "The Son of Man came . . . to give his life as a ransom for many" (Mark 10:45). "The Son of Man came to seek and to save the lost" (Luke 19:10). "I have not come to call the righteous but sinners to repentance" (Luke 5:32). "I came that they may have life and have it abundantly" (John 10:10). "What shall I say? 'Father, save me from this hour'? But for this purpose I have come to this hour. Father, glorify your name" (John 12:27-28).

In summary, then, he came to "die for the nation [of Israel], and not for the nation only, but also to gather into one the children of God who are scattered abroad" (John 11:51-52). He came to *gather* a people—specifically, to gather a people in allegiance to himself for the glory of his Father—by dying to save them from their sins and to give them eternal life and a new ethic of love like his (John 13:34-35). Therefore, when he demands that we follow him, he means that we join him in that task of gathering: "Whoever does not *gather* with

me scatters" (Luke 11:23). There are no neutral
followers; we either scatter or gather. Following
Jesus means continuing the work he came to do—
gathering a people in allegiance to him for the glory
of his Father.

FOLLOWING JESUS INTO SUFFERING

Continuing the work he came to do even includes
the suffering he came to do. Following Jesus means
that we share in his suffering. When Jesus calls us to
follow him, this is where he puts the emphasis. He
knows he is heading to the cross, and he demands
that we do the same. He designs his entire life and
ministry to go to Jerusalem and be killed. "I must
go on my way today and tomorrow and the day
following, for it cannot be that a prophet should
perish away from Jerusalem" (Luke 13:33).

So he "set his face to go to Jerusalem" (Luke
9:51). And he knew exactly what would happen
there. It was all planned by his Father when he sent
him into the world. "See, we are going up to Jerusalem, and the Son of Man will be delivered over to the
chief priests and the scribes, and they will condemn
him to death and deliver him over to the Gentiles.

And they will mock him and spit on him, and flog him and kill him. And after three days he will rise" (Mark 10:33-34). That's the plan—down to the details of being spit on.

That was the design of his life. And he knew that his own pain would also fall on those who followed him. "If they persecuted me, they will also persecute you" (John 15:20). So the unflinching focus of his demand was that we follow him in suffering. "If anyone would come after me, let him deny himself and take up his cross and follow me" (Matt. 16:24). Jesus put the emphasis on self-denial and cross-bearing.

SUFFERING FOR JESUS WITH JOY
SHOWS HIS SUPREME VALUE

He did not die to make this life easy for us or prosperous. He died to remove every obstacle to our everlasting joy in making much of him. And he calls us to follow him in his sufferings because this life of joyful suffering for Jesus' sake (Matt. 5:12) shows that he is more valuable than all the earthly rewards that the world lives for (Matt. 13:44; 6:19-20). If you follow Jesus only because he makes life easy now, it will look to the world as though you really love

what they love, and Jesus just happens to provide it
for you. But if you suffer with Jesus in the pathway
of love because he is your supreme treasure, then it
will be apparent to the world that your heart is set
on a different fortune than theirs. This is why Jesus
demands that we deny ourselves and take up our
cross and follow him.

Suffering for Jesus Is Temporary; Pleasure in Jesus Is Eternal

Of course, the pain is temporary. He does not call us
to eternal suffering. That's what he rescues us from.
"Whoever loves his life loses it, and whoever hates
his life *in this world* will keep it for *eternal life*"
(John 12:25). "Whoever loses his life for my sake
and the gospel's will *save* it" (Mark 8:35). Suffering
for Jesus is temporary. Pleasure in Jesus is eternal.
When Peter said (perhaps with a tinge of self-pity),
"See, we have left everything and followed you,"
Jesus responded, without coddling Peter's self-pity,
"Everyone who has left houses or brothers or sisters or father or mother or children or lands, for my
name's sake, will receive a hundredfold and will
inherit eternal life" (Matt. 19:27, 29). In other words,

there is no ultimate sacrifice in following Jesus. "You will be repaid at the resurrection of the just" (Luke 14:14). "Your reward is great in heaven" (Matt. 5:12).

Even before heaven, joy abounds along the hard road that leads through death to resurrection. Nothing can compare with the joy of walking in the light with Jesus as opposed to walking in the darkness without him. Jesus said, "I am the light of the world. Whoever follows me will not walk in darkness, but will have the light of life" (John 8:12). Following Jesus does indeed lead through suffering and death. But the path is luminous with life and truth. Jesus promised, "I am with you always, to the end of the age" (Matt. 28:20). And where Jesus is present there is joy—joy in sorrow for now, but joy nevertheless. "These things I have spoken to you, that my joy may be in you, and that your joy may be full" (John 15:11).

RUPTURES IN RELATIONSHIPS WITH PEOPLE

This is why the ruptures caused by following Jesus are not devastating. There are ruptures in relationships with people, relationships with possessions, and relationships with our vocation.

Jesus has jolting ways of describing the cost of following him in relation to people. "Follow me, and leave the dead to bury their own dead" (Matt. 8:22). "If anyone comes to me and does not hate his own father and mother and wife and children and brothers and sisters, yes, and even his own life, he cannot be my disciple" (Luke 14:26). In other words, following Jesus is so supremely important that it calls for behaviors that are sometimes going to look like *hate* to the world. I have seen this lived out in agonizing choices that missionaries make to take their little children to risky places and leave aging parents behind, well cared for but perhaps never to be seen on earth again. Some call it loveless. But Jesus has his eyes on the nations and what love demands in their case.

Ruptures in Relationships with Possessions
Following Jesus also ruptures our relationship with possessions. There once was a rich young man who loved his possessions too much. So Jesus cut to the heart of his idolatry with the demand, "If you would be perfect, go, sell what you possess and give to the poor, and you will have treasure in heaven; and

come, follow me" (Matt. 19:21). If something gets in the way of following Jesus, we must get rid of it.

And this is not unique to that rich man but applies to all of us: "*Any one* of you who does not renounce all that he has cannot be my disciple" (Luke 14:33). Renouncing what you have may not always mean selling it all. Jesus commended Zacchaeus for giving *half* of his goods to the poor (Luke 19:8-9). But renouncing *all* does mean that everything we have is totally at Jesus' disposal for purposes that please him and that it must never get in the way of radical obedience to his command of love.

RUPTURES IN RELATIONSHIPS WITH VOCATION
Then there is the rupture that following Jesus brings to our vocation. When Jesus called the twelve to follow him, none of them was a professional Jesus-follower. They were fishermen and tax collectors and the like. They had jobs. Incredibly, it went something like this: "As [Jesus] passed by, he saw Levi the son of Alphaeus sitting at the tax booth, and he said to him, 'Follow me.' And he rose and followed him" (Mark 2:14). Just like that! (As far as we know.) For most of us it was not that simple. But it does happen.

And it may happen to you. Not everyone should leave his vocation to follow Jesus. When one man wanted to leave his homeland and follow Jesus, Jesus said, "Go home to your friends and tell them how much the Lord has done for you, and how he has had mercy on you" (Mark 5:19). Most of us should stay where we are and follow Jesus in all the radical ways of love demanded by our present position and relationships.[1] But not everyone. For some—perhaps for you (even as you read this)—following Jesus will mean a risky rupture in your vocation. Do not be afraid to follow him away from the familiar.

FOLLOWING JESUS IS COSTLY AND WORTH IT

Jesus has no desire to trick you into following him with a kind of bait and switch. He is utterly up front about the cost. In fact, he urges you to count the cost. "For which of you, desiring to build a tower, does not first sit down and count the cost, whether he has enough to complete it? . . . Or what king, going out to encounter another king in war, will not sit down first and deliberate whether he is able with ten thousand to meet him who comes against him with twenty thousand?" (Luke 14:28, 31). Let the call to follow

Jesus be clear and honest. "In the world you will have tribulation. But take heart; I have overcome the world" (John 16:33). It is costly, and it is worth it.

Blessed are you when people hate you and when they exclude you and revile you and spurn your name as evil, on account of the Son of Man! Rejoice in that day, and leap for joy, for behold, your reward is great in heaven; for so their fathers did to the prophets.

LUKE 6:22-23

Behold, I have given you authority to tread on serpents and scorpions, and over all the power of the enemy, and nothing shall hurt you. Nevertheless, do not rejoice in this, that the spirits are subject to you, but rejoice that your names are written in heaven.

LUKE 10:19-20

The kingdom of heaven is like treasure hidden in a field, which a man found and covered up. Then in his joy he goes and sells all that he has and buys that field.

MATTHEW 13:44

These things I have spoken to you, that my joy may be in you, and that your joy may be full.

JOHN 15:11

Chapter Three

The Road Is Hard,
But It Is Not Joyless

The road is hard that leads through death to
resurrection. And Jesus commands us to follow
him on it. Therefore, it is remarkable that he also
commands us to rejoice and leap for joy on our
journey.

Surprised by Joy

Jesus' demand that we "rejoice . . . and leap for joy"
(Luke 6:23; cf. Matt. 5:12) is astonishing for so many
reasons that it would take whole books to unfold all of
its surprising implications.[1] Half a century ago C. S.
Lewis responded to this surprise by looking at the
inescapable evidence in the Gospels. He wrote:

> If we consider the unblushing promises of reward
> and the staggering nature of the rewards promised in
> the Gospels, it would seem that our Lord finds our
> desires not too strong, but too weak. We are half-
> hearted creatures, fooling about with drink and sex
> and ambition when infinite joy is offered us, like an

ignorant child who wants to go on making mud pies
in a slum because he cannot imagine what is meant
by the offer of a holiday at the sea. We are far too
easily pleased.[2]

In other words, the demand that we be happy is not
marginal or superfluous. It is a shocking wake-up call
to people who are finding their happiness in all the
wrong places. Jesus' solution to our love affair with
sin is not merely that we tear out our sin-loving eyes
(Matt. 5:29) but that we be mastered by joy in a new
reality, namely, God.

IN HIS JOY HE GOES AND SELLS ALL THAT HE HAS
Central to his preaching was the announcement that
the kingdom of heaven had come near. He meant that
he was the King and that his work was the arrival of
the saving rule of God (Luke 11:20; 17:20-21). So he
told a very short parable to show how people come
into the kingdom. He said, "The kingdom of heaven
is like treasure hidden in a field, which a man found
and covered up. Then *in his joy* he goes and sells all
that he has and buys that field" (Matt. 13:44).

The parable means that God's saving presence
and sovereign reign are so valuable that when people

see them for what they really are—treasure hidden in the field—they count everything as nothing compared to the vast fortune of being part of that reign. And Jesus leaves no doubt about the internal experience of that "conversion." It is joy-driven. He says, "*In his joy* he goes and sells all that he has and buys that field."

It cannot be otherwise. Jesus came into the world with *good* news, not bad news. He does not call us to a willpower religion that feels only duty and no delight. He calls us to himself and to his Father. Therefore, he calls us to joy. Of course, it is not joy in things. Jesus is not preaching a health, wealth, and prosperity gospel—one of America's most lamentable exports to the world. It is joy in *God* and in his *Son*.

This is why the parable describes coming to the kingdom as "selling all." The demand for joy does not encourage us to retreat one millimeter from the radical demand of Luke 14:33, "Any one of you who does not renounce all that he has cannot be my disciple." We renounce all those joy-giving things because we have found the treasure hidden in the field and we have been given eyes to see that this treasure—this glorious God—is infinitely more valuable than everything we possess or could possess in this world. This is why we renounce it all with joy.

SELF-DENIAL AND THE QUEST FOR JOY

This is the meaning of self-denial. Renounce everything on earth in order that you might have Jesus. Sell all, so that you might have the kingdom. C. S. Lewis captures the spirit of Jesus' demand for self-denial when he says:

> The New Testament has lots to say about self-denial, but not about self-denial as an end in itself. We are told to deny ourselves and to take up our crosses in order that we may follow Christ; and nearly every description of what we shall ultimately find if we do so contains an appeal to desire.[3]

In other words, we deny ourselves because beyond self-denial is great reward. Jonathan Edwards goes even deeper in his analysis of how Jesus' demand for self-denial relates to his demand for joy.

> Self-denial will also be reckoned amongst the troubles of the godly. . . . But whoever has tried self-denial can give in his testimony that they never experience greater pleasure and joys than after great

acts of self-denial. Self-denial destroys the very
root and foundation of sorrow, and is nothing else
but the lancing of a grievous and painful sore that
effects a cure and brings abundance of health as a
recompense for the pain of the operation.[4]

If this is true, then Jesus' demand for self-denial is
another way of calling us to radically pursue our
deepest and most lasting joy. They are not competing
commands. They are like the command to be cancer-
free and the command to have surgery.

OUR JOY IS NOT MAINLY IN PROSPERITY BUT IN OBEDIENCE AND PAIN

What astonishes us most immediately when Jesus
says, "Rejoice . . . and leap for joy" is that he is
saying it precisely in the context of pain. "Blessed
are you when people hate you and when they exclude
you and revile you and spurn your name as evil, on
account of the Son of Man! Rejoice in that day, and
leap for joy" (Luke 6:22-23). When Jesus demands
that we rejoice, he has not forgotten the kind of
world we live in. It is filled with suffering. And he
promises that some of that suffering will fall on us as
his disciples. "They will lay their hands on you and

persecute you, delivering you up to the synagogues
and prisons . . . and some of you they will put to
death. You will be hated by all for my name's sake"
(Luke 21:12, 16-17). "If they have called the master
of the house Beelzebul, how much more will they
malign those of his household" (Matt. 10:25). "If
they persecuted me, they will also persecute you"
(John 15:20).

Jesus has not forgotten that. In fact, he demands
that we follow him in that painful path of love.
Therefore, the joy he demands now ("in that day,"
Luke 6:23) is not chipper. It is not joy-lite. It is not
superficial or marked with levity. This is the mistake
of too many people and too many churches. They
think that Jesus' demand for joy is a demand to tell
jokes or weave slapstick into Christian corporate
life. I don't smell the Jerusalem-bound Jesus in that
atmosphere. Something has gone wrong.

What's wrong is that the aroma of suffering is
missing. For Jesus, the demand for joy is a way to
live with suffering and to outlast suffering. Therefore,
this joy is serious. It's the kind you fight for by
cutting off your hand (Matt. 5:30) and selling your
possessions (Matt. 13:44) and carrying a cross with

Jesus to Calvary (Matt. 10:38-39). It has scars. It sings happy songs with tears. It remembers the dark hours and knows that more are coming. The road to heaven is a hard road, but it is not joyless.

THE ROOT OF HOLINESS

Jesus' demand that we rejoice is the key that unlocks his demand for holiness. What chokes the purifying power of spiritual life and destroys Jesus' would-be disciples are the "cares and riches and pleasures of life" (Luke 8:14). And what severs these strangling vines most decisively is the power of a superior pleasure. Jesus said that it is "in his joy" that the believer sells everything. In other words, it is his joy that cuts the stranglehold of sin.

Many Christians think stoicism is a good antidote to sensuality. It isn't. It is hopelessly weak and ineffective. Willpower religion usually fails, and even when it succeeds, it gets glory for the will, not for God. It produces legalists, not lovers. Jonathan Edwards saw the powerlessness of this approach and said:

> We come with double forces against the wicked, to persuade them to a godly life. . . . The common

> argument is the profitableness of religion, but alas,
> the wicked man is not in pursuit of [moral] profit;
> 'tis pleasure he seeks. Now, then, we will fight with
> them with their own weapons.[5]

In other words, the pursuit of pleasure in God is not a
compromise with the sensual world but is in fact the
only power that can defeat the lusts of the age while
producing lovers of God.

THE ROOT OF JOY IN SUFFERING
IS GREAT REWARD: JESUS

Jesus bases our present joy explicitly on the hope for
great reward. "Rejoice in that day, and leap for joy,
for behold, *your reward is great in heaven*" (Luke
6:23). He does not define the reward. But in the
whole context of his life and message, the essential
reward is fellowship with Jesus himself and with God
the Father through him (John 17:3, 24).

There are several pointers to this understanding.
For example, Jesus says to his disciples just before
his death, "You have sorrow now, but *I will see
you again* and your hearts will rejoice, and no one
will take your joy from you" (John 16:22). The
indomitable joy that Jesus promises is based on his

own presence: "I will see you again."

Similarly Jesus says, "These things I have spoken to you, that my joy may be in you, and that your joy may be full" (John 15:11). This fullness of joy is mentioned by John the Baptist, and he bases it on the presence of Jesus, comparing Jesus to a bridegroom and himself to his friend: "The friend of the bridegroom, who stands and hears him, *rejoices greatly at the bridegroom's voice*. Therefore this joy of mine is now complete" (John 3:29).[6] John's "complete" joy is based on the presence of Jesus.

Therefore, I conclude that the essence of the reward that we count on to complete our joy is the fullness of the presence of Jesus experienced in the age to come. The reason that we can rejoice now is not only that we taste that future fellowship in hope, but also that Jesus is with us now by his Spirit. He promised us, as he left to return to the Father, "I will not leave you as orphans; I will come to you" (John 14:18). "I am with you always, to the end of the age" (Matt. 28:20). He said that the Spirit of truth would come and make Jesus gloriously real to us even though he is physically absent. "When the Spirit of truth comes, he will . . . glorify me, for he will take what is mine and declare it to you" (John 16:13-14). Therefore, even though we can't see Jesus *now*, we hope in him with great joy, and he sustains that joy by his continual presence.

Jesus Purchases and Provides Our Joy

How then shall we obey this demand of Jesus to "rejoice . . . and leap for joy"? We will take heart from the fact that Jesus offered himself to die for the forgiveness of our sins—the forgiveness of our failures to rejoice in him as we ought. At the Last Supper he took the cup of wine and said, "This is my blood of the covenant, which is poured out for many *for the forgiveness of sins*" (Matt. 26:28). This is why he came in the first place: "The Son of Man came . . . to give his life as a ransom for many" (Mark 10:45). So our joy has this solid foundation: Jesus shed his blood so that our failures to rejoice in him might be forgiven.

Then we take heart that he promised to work for us in such a way that the very love that the Father has for the Son would be the experience of our own hearts. He prayed, "I made known to them your name, and I will continue to make it known, that the love with which you have loved me may be in them, and I in them" (John 17:26). Consider carefully that the love the Father has for the Son is not a merciful, forgiving love. The Son has no sin and no flaw. He needs no mercy. The love the Father has for the Son is nothing but infinitely joyful admiration and fellowship. This is what Jesus says will be in us. Therefore, I take this to be a promise to work in us to make sure that our joy will be the very joy that the Father has in the Son. We are not left to ourselves to rejoice in Jesus as we ought. Jesus is committed to making it happen.

THE DEMAND TO REJOICE IN JESUS AS A MEANS TO GLORIFY JESUS

Finally, I conclude from Jesus' commitment to glorify the Father and the Son (John 17:1) that his intention to sustain our joy in him is part of what it means for us to glorify the Father and the Son. In other words, I conclude that rejoicing in the Father and the Son is essential to glorifying God. If this is true, we have a powerful confirmation of the duty to pursue our joy—namely, because it displays the glory of God.

This truth should make us tremble at the horror of not rejoicing in God. We should quake at the fearful lukewarmness of our hearts. We should waken to the truth that it is a treacherous sin not to pursue our fullest satisfaction in God. There is one final word for finding delight in the creation more than in the Creator: *treason*. What a motivation this should be to obey the demand of Jesus, "Rejoice . . . and leap for joy."

THERE IS NO LIMIT TO THE INTENSITY OF JOY IN JESUS

It is true that a passion for happiness can be misdirected to wrong objects, but it cannot be too strong. Jonathan Edwards argued for this in a sermon that he preached on Song of Solomon 5:1. The text reads, "Eat, friends, drink, and be drunk with love!" Edwards drew out of the text the following doctrine: "Persons need not and ought not to set any bounds to their spiritual and gracious appetites." Instead, he says, they ought

> to be endeavoring by all possible ways to inflame their desires and to obtain more spiritual pleasures. . . . Our hungerings and thirstings after

God and Jesus Christ and after holiness can't be
too great for the value of these things, for they are
things of infinite value. . . . [Therefore] endeavor
to promote spiritual appetites by laying yourself in
the way of allurement. . . . There is no such thing as
excess in our taking of this spiritual food. There is
no such virtue as temperance in spiritual feasting.[7]

Therefore, be encouraged that God made you to
rejoice in him. Do not settle for any lesser joy. Lay
yourself in the way of allurement. That is, fix your
eyes on the all-satisfying treasure of Jesus Christ who
loved us and gave his life as a ransom for our everlasting joy.

Part Two:

Jesus, Joy, and Striving to Enter the Kingdom

And someone said to him, "Lord, will those who are saved be few?" And he said to them, "Strive to enter through the narrow door. For many, I tell you, will seek to enter and will not be able."

LUKE 13:23-24

CHAPTER FOUR

STRIVE TO ENTER
THE NARROW DOOR

Jesus taught us that life is war. When he said, *"Strive* to enter through the narrow door" (Luke 13:24), the Greek word behind the English "strive" is recognizable in English transliteration: *agōnizesthe*. You can see the word *agonize* in that Greek word. The implication is that we must struggle, wrestle, and exert ourselves. But the most important fact about the word "strive" is that the one other place where we find it on Jesus' lips is John 18:36, where he says his disciples would be "fighting" if his kingdom were of this world. "My kingdom is not of this world. If my kingdom were of this world, my servants *would have been fighting* [*ēgōnizonto*], that I might not be delivered over to the Jews." So here the phrase "strive to enter" means that entering is a battle.

STRIVE TO ENTER WHAT?

Entering what? The kingdom of God. This is plain
from the following context. After saying that we
should "strive to enter through the narrow door,"
he refers to a master of a house who rises and shuts
the door so that no one else can enter (Luke 13:25).
Those outside knock and say, "Lord, open to us,"
but the master says, "I do not know where you come
from." Then they say, "We ate and drank in your
presence, and you taught in our streets." But he
responds, "Depart from me, all you workers of evil!"
(Luke 13:25-27).

Then Jesus applies this picture to the real
situation of some who will be excluded from the
kingdom of God while Gentiles from all over the
world will "recline at table in the kingdom of God."
"In that place there will be weeping and gnashing of
teeth, when you see Abraham and Isaac and Jacob
and all the prophets *in the kingdom of God* but you
yourselves cast out. And people will come from east
and west, and from north and south, and recline at
table *in the kingdom of God*" (Luke 13:28-29).

So the "narrow door" through which we must
"strive" to enter is the door to the kingdom of God.

Outside there is "weeping and gnashing of teeth" (Luke 13:28). This is one of the ways Jesus refers to hell: "Throw them into the fiery furnace. In that place there will be weeping and gnashing of teeth" (Matt. 13:50). The alternative to entering by the narrow gate is destruction. "Enter by the narrow gate. For the gate is wide and the way is easy that leads to *destruction*" (Matt. 7:13). In other words, what is at stake when Jesus demands that we "strive to enter" is heaven and hell. It is an ultimate issue.

THE GREATEST THREAT IS OUR OWN SIN EVERY DAY

But what does Jesus want us to strive against so that we can enter through the narrow door? What are the obstacles? If life is war, who is the enemy? In our striving, the aim is not to hurt anyone. Jesus is clear that we are to love our enemies and do good to those who hate us (Luke 6:27). Saying that life is war does not mean that we make war on people, but on sin, especially our own. In fact, it is only our own sin that can keep us from entering the kingdom, not anyone else's. The sin of others can hurt us, even kill us. But that does not keep us from entering the kingdom of

God. Our own sin is the greatest threat to entering the kingdom of God. But temptation to sin comes from an amazing variety of sources.

Jesus is demanding serious personal vigilance. The command to "watch" is one of his most frequent commands. The idea is that we must be awake and alert and ready, lest the temptations of life take us off guard and we be overcome and ruined. Jesus said to his disciples in the Garden of Gethsemane, "Watch and pray that you may not enter into temptation. The spirit indeed is willing, but the flesh is weak" (Mark 14:38). This command is relevant to all of life. Temptations abound, and Jesus does not take them lightly. The watchword of all of life is, watch, be alert.

I say *all of life* because Jesus warned that the days just before his second coming would be in many ways very normal. It will be, Jesus says, like the days of Noah before the flood came and swept people away who were utterly unsuspecting. They were not watchful. Life seemed too normal, so they were not vigilant. "As in those days before the flood they were eating and drinking, marrying and giving in marriage, until the day when Noah entered the ark . . . so will be the coming of the Son of Man. . . . Therefore, *stay awake*, for you do not know on what day your Lord is coming" (Matt. 24:38-39, 42). Nothing is more normal than eating and drinking and marrying. The point is that we must be vigilant all the time, not just when the times feel perilous. They are always perilous. Soul destroying temptations to unbelief and sin are present in everyday, normal life. Striving to enter through the narrow door is a lifelong, all-day, every-day calling.

PAIN AND PLEASURE CAN KEEP US FROM ENTERING THROUGH THE NARROW DOOR

Jesus' demand for vigilance is all-embracing. Both the pleasant parts of life and the painful parts of life present dangers to the soul. In the parable of the four soils he warns about both. The painful and the pleasant threaten to destroy the faith-sustaining work of the word in our lives. When the word falls on rocky ground, it sprouts, then dies. This represents those who hear the word, but then "tribulation or persecution arises on account of the word" (Matt. 13:21), and they fall away. They do not enter through the narrow door.

When the word falls on thorny ground, it sprouts, then dies. This represents those who hear the word, but then "they are choked by the cares and riches and pleasures of life" (Luke 8:14). They do not enter through the narrow door. One person falls away because of pain (tribulation or persecution); the other person falls away because of pleasure (riches and pleasures of life). The call for vigilance is all-embracing. There is no unembattled place in this life.

Surprising to us perhaps, Jesus' demand for vigilance is directed more often at the pleasures of life than the pain. Some people are driven away from God by their pain, but more are lured away by their pleasures. Pleasures seldom awaken people to their need for God; pain often does. So Jesus is more concerned to warn us about the dangers of prosperity than the dangers of poverty.

THE PERILS OF PRAISE AND PHYSICAL INDULGENCE
One powerful lure away from the kingdom of God is the praise of man. Therefore, Jesus said, "Beware of the scribes, who like to walk around in long robes, and love greetings in the marketplaces and the best seats in the synagogues and the places of honor

at feasts" (Luke 20:46). "Beware" means be alert, take care, pay close attention to. This is a call for vigilance against the lure of following those who live for the praises of man. "Beware of practicing your righteousness before other people in order to be seen by them" (Matt. 6:1). We feel good when people speak well of us. It may not be wrong. But it is dangerous. It is a time for vigilance. "Woe to you," Jesus says, "when all people speak well of you, for so their fathers did to the false prophets" (Luke 6:26).

Less subtle is the lure of physical indulgence. Jesus focuses on alcohol and the dissipating effects it has on our minds and bodies. He says, "But watch yourselves lest your hearts be weighed down with dissipation and drunkenness and cares of this life, and that day come upon you suddenly like a trap" (Luke 21:34). There are drugs and foods and practices that "weigh down" the heart. They make the heart sluggish. This is the opposite of vigilance. We will not "strive to enter through the narrow door" if we are self-indulgent and use drugs or food or drink in a way that dulls our spiritual alertness and vigilance.

MONEY IS A MORTAL THREAT TO ENTERING THROUGH THE NARROW DOOR

The danger Jesus warns against most often is the danger of money. It is a mortal danger. Heaven and hell hang in the balance in our vigilance against the lure of money. Jesus made this as clear as possible with the words, "It is easier for a camel to go through the eye of a needle than for a rich person to enter the kingdom of God" (Mark 10:25). The issue is entering the kingdom. Striving for wealth is not the striving that leads to the narrow door.

Over and over Jesus warns us to be vigilant against the lure of riches. "Do not lay up for yourselves treasures on earth" (Matt. 6:19). "You cannot serve God and money" (Matt. 6:24). "Do not be anxious, saying, 'What shall we eat?' or 'What shall we drink?' or 'What shall we wear?'" (Matt. 6:31). "The deceitfulness of riches and the desires for other things enter in and choke the word" (Mark 4:19). "Sell your possessions, and give to the needy" (Luke 12:33). "Where your treasure is, there your heart will be also" (Matt. 6:21). "Any one of you who does not renounce all that he has cannot be my disciple" (Luke 14:33). "But woe to you who are rich, for you have received your consolation" (Luke 6:24). "Blessed are you who are poor, for yours is the kingdom of God" (Luke 6:20).[1] "Take care, and be on your guard against all covetousness, for one's life does not consist in the abundance of his possessions" (Luke 12:15).

THE "HEALTHY EYE" WILL HELP US STRIVE TO ENTER THE NARROW DOOR

It appears, then, that striving to enter the kingdom of God through the narrow door is largely a battle about how we relate to money. We should linger here since Jesus did. He is jealous that we "guard against all covetousness." He is deeply concerned with our "eyes" when it comes to the treasure of our lives. We see this in a puzzling statement he made in Matthew 6:22-23, "The eye is the lamp of the body. So, if your eye is healthy, your whole body will be full of light, but if your eye is bad, your whole body will be full of darkness. If then the light in you is darkness, how great is the darkness!" In other words, if the eye is good (literally, "single"), the whole body will be full of light. But if the eye is bad, the body will be full of darkness. In other words, how you see reality determines whether you are in the dark or not.

You will naturally ask, what does that have to do with money? First of all, notice that these words of Jesus are sandwiched between the command to lay up treasures in heaven (6:19-21) and the warning that you can't serve God and money (6:24). Why is this saying about the good and bad eye sandwiched between two teachings on money? I think it's because what makes the eye good is how it sees God in relation to money. That's the issue on either side of this saying. In Matthew 6:19-21 the issue is: You should desire heaven-reward, not earth-reward. Which, in short, means: Desire God, not money. In Matthew 6:24, the question is whether you can serve two masters. Answer: You cannot serve God and money.

This is a double description of light! If you are laying up treasures in heaven, not earth, you are walking in the light. If you are serving God, not money, you are walking in the light. Between these two descriptions of the light, Jesus says that the eye is the lamp of the body and that a good eye produces a fullness of this light. So, what is the

good eye that gives so much light and the bad eye
that leaves us in the dark?

What Is the Good Eye?

One clue is found in Matthew 20:15. Jesus has just
said that men who worked one hour will be paid
the same as those who worked all day, because
the master is merciful and generous. And besides,
they all agreed to their wages before they worked.
Those who worked all day grumbled that the men
who worked one hour were paid too much. Jesus
responded with the same words found here in
Matthew 6:23, "Is your eye bad because I am good?"
(literal translation).

What is bad about their eye? What's bad is that
their eye does not see the mercy of the master as
beautiful. They see it as ugly. They don't see reality
for what it is. They do not have an eye that can see
mercy as more precious than money.

Now bring that understanding of the "bad eye"
back to Matthew 6:23 and let it help us discern the
meaning of the "good eye." What would the good
eye be that fills us with light? It would be an eye that
sees the Master's generosity as more precious than

money. Which means that the good eye sees God and his ways as the great Treasure in life, not money. The good eye sees things as they really are. God is really more valuable than all that money can buy.

You have a good eye if you look to God and love to maximize the reward of his fellowship—that is, lay up treasure in heaven. You have a good eye if you look at Master-money and Master-God and see Master-God as infinitely more valuable. In other words, a "good eye" is a wisely valuing eye, a discerning eye, an astutely treasuring eye. It doesn't just see facts about money and God. It doesn't just perceive what is true and false. It sees beauty and ugliness; it senses value and worthlessness; it discerns what is really desirable and what is undesirable. The seeing of the good eye is not neutral. When it sees God, it sees God-as-beautiful. It sees God-as-desirable.

That is why the good eye leads to the way of light: laying up treasures in heaven and serving God, not money. The good eye is a *single* eye. It has *one* Treasure: God. When that happens in your life, you are full of light. And this is so important that Jesus adds in Luke 11:35, "Therefore *be careful* lest the light in you be darkness." In other words, be vigilant. Don't be casual or slack or careless about this matter. Strive, wrestle, fight to keep your eye good. That is, do what you must to see God, not money, as supremely valuable and desirable.

In the next chapter, we will continue to unfold the implications of Jesus' demand to strive to enter by the narrow door. We will see how he calls for vigilance and watchfulness in regard to false prophets and false christs and the suddenness of his second coming. And then we will turn to the question, how does the demand for vigilance fit with his demand that we rest in him? How does the seriousness of watchfulness fit with the sweetness of Jesus' care?

Enter by the narrow gate. For the gate is wide and the way is easy that leads to destruction, and those who enter by it are many. For the gate is narrow and the way is hard that leads to life, and those who find it are few.

<small>MATTHEW 7:13-14</small>

This cup that is poured out for you is the new covenant in my blood.

<small>LUKE 22:20</small>

CHAPTER FIVE

WITHOUT JESUS OUR STRIVING WOULD BE LOSING

Jesus' demand for vigilance—"strive to enter through the narrow door"—is owing to the many dangers that threaten our souls. One of the most frequent imperatives on Jesus' lips is, "Look out!" "Watch!" "Be alert!" We have seen in the previous chapter the need for striving against the perils of pain and pleasure: the deceit of money, the praise of man, the lure of physical indulgence. We turn now to the perils of false prophets and false christs and the danger of nostalgia for the days when the cost of discipleship was not so high. Then we turn to the crucial question: Is all this vigilance and all this striving to enter through the narrow door consistent with the sweet invitations of Jesus to come to him and find rest?

THE PERILS OF FALSE PROPHETS AND FALSE CHRISTS

Jesus warns us that false prophets and even false christs will abound. In fact, the first warning he gives

us after saying, "The gate is narrow and the way
is hard that leads to life" is this: "Beware of false
prophets, who come to you in sheep's clothing but
inwardly are ravenous wolves. You will recognize
them by their fruits" (Matt. 7:15-16). This is not a
casual remark. It is a life-and-death warning: "False
christs and false prophets will arise and perform signs
and wonders, to lead astray, if possible, the elect. *But
be on guard*; I have told you all things beforehand"
(Mark 13:22-23). Be on guard! Keep your eyes open!
Watch! Be vigilant! Strive to enter by the narrow
door.

Jesus underscores that the door is *narrow* that
leads to life. Not every claim will fit through the
narrow door of the kingdom of God. There are many
false christs. In this context *Christ* means Jewish
Messiah—the one who fulfills all God's promises
and brings in the kingdom and sits on the throne of
David, ruling over all the world. There is only one
Christ, and the rest are "false christs." Jesus is the
only Messiah. Therefore, the door is as narrow as
faith in Jesus, the only true Messiah and King of
kings.

I have sat in my office with followers of another

"christ" and pleaded with them to turn to the true and only Christ, Jesus. They said that the Christ had come in our day and that he was gathering a people now for himself. I read to them Luke 17:24 to show them that Jesus said when he comes it would be globally unmistakable and that anyone who says it has already happened is a pretender: "For as the lightning flashes and lights up the sky from one side to the other, so will the Son of Man be in his day." They said that in order to understand the secret meaning of this verse I would need to read a book written by their leader, the "christ" they believed in. As they left I stood at my window watching them walk across the parking lot and prayed for them. I gave thanks that God had helped me "be on guard." Jesus said this would happen and helped me watch as I sat there in my office. This vigilance is part of what it means to "strive to enter through the narrow door."

YOU DO NOT KNOW WHEN YOUR LORD IS COMING

What gives Jesus' demand for vigilance and striving its unusual urgency is the warning that the time of his second coming is unknown to any of us. "*Stay awake*, for you do not know on what day your Lord is coming. . . . *Watch* therefore, for you know neither the day nor the hour" (Matt. 24:42; 25:13). When Jesus tells us to "watch" or "stay awake" because we do not know the time of his second coming, he does not mean that we skip sleep and look out our windows. We know this because the command to "watch" is the climax of the parable of the ten virgins, five of whom were wise and five of whom were foolish, but all of whom slept. The wise made sure they had oil in their lamps so that when the bridegroom came they might go out with their lamps to greet him. That was their job. Jesus says that all ten of them "became drowsy and slept" (Matt. 25:5). He did not criticize the wise virgins for sleeping.

When the bridegroom came at midnight (representing the second coming of Jesus to earth at an unexpected hour), Jesus said, "Those who were ready [the five wise virgins] went in with him to the marriage feast, and the door was shut" (Matt. 25:10). The foolish virgins had to go get oil because they were unprepared. When they returned they cried out, "Lord, lord, open to us" (Matt. 25:11). But the bridegroom (representing Jesus) answered, "Truly,

I say to you, I do not know you" (Matt. 25:12). The lesson Jesus draws out of this parable is, "Watch therefore, for you know neither the day nor the hour" (Matt. 25:13). But all ten of the virgins were asleep, including the five wise virgins. That's how we know that when Jesus says, "Watch!" he does not mean skipping sleep and looking out our window.

He means, be watchful over your life. Be watchful over what the Bridegroom has called you to do. The wise virgins had done the will of the Master: Their lamps were fully prepared. Sleeping was just fine because they had done their jobs. Therefore, one way to describe "striving to enter through the narrow door" is: Fulfill your calling. Be vigilant to do what God has called you to do. You will be happy if Jesus comes and finds you heartily engaged in your earthly calling for his glory. "Who then is the faithful and wise manager, whom his master will set over his household, to give them their portion of food at the proper time? Blessed is that servant whom his master will find so doing when he comes" (Luke 12:42-3). Striving to enter the kingdom by the narrow door includes vigilant faithfulness in the work Jesus has left us to do. As he said in one of his parables,

"Engage in business until I come" (Luke 19:13)—do with all your might what he has given you to do.

Perseverance and the Peril of Nostalgia

One of the great temptations to keep us from fulfilling what Jesus calls us to do is that we grow weary in the battle and look back on how easy life was before we started to follow him. Strive to enter through the narrow door means, fight for perseverance. The zeal of many would-be followers of Jesus grows cold, and they drift away. Jesus said, "Because lawlessness will be increased, the love of many will grow cold. But the one who endures to the end will be saved" (Matt. 24:12-13). In other words, one of the factors that makes the door to the kingdom of God narrow is that striving to enter must last to the end.

Therefore, Jesus warns us against nostalgia for the former days of worldliness. He says that the stress of the last days of this age will tempt people to look back. So with stark simplicity he warns, "Remember Lot's wife" (Luke 17:32). This was a reference to a woman in the Old Testament who was leaving her hometown of Sodom because God was about to destroy the city for its sin. Tragically, like so many would-be followers of Jesus who begin to leave the old way of sin, she looked back. "Lot's wife . . . looked back, and she became a pillar of salt" (Gen. 19:26). God saw an idolatrous heart in her backward glance toward Sodom. This was her true love, not God. Striving to enter through the narrow door means taking heed to the warning of Jesus: "No one who puts his hand to the plow and looks back is fit for the kingdom of God" (Luke 9:62).

How Does Striving to Enter by the Narrow Door Relate to Resting in Jesus?

The question must now be asked: Is all this vigilance and all this striving to enter through the narrow door consistent with the sweet invitations of Jesus to come to him and find rest? If this striving and vigilance sounds like a miserable and burdened way to live, keep in mind that Jesus rebuked the lawyers who burdened people with impossible laws without giving any help: "Woe to you lawyers also! For you load people with burdens hard to bear, and you yourselves do not touch the burdens with one of your fingers" (Luke 11:46). And most of all, keep in mind how Jesus invited people into his fellowship: "Come to me, all who labor and are heavy laden, and I will give you rest. Take my yoke upon you, and learn from me, for I am gentle and lowly in heart, and you will find rest for your souls. For my yoke is easy, and my burden is light" (Matt. 11:28-30).

What makes the demands of Jesus to strive and to be vigilant seem burdensome is the assumption that we are left to ourselves. Our natural tendency is to think that if Jesus tells us to do something and makes this a condition for entering the kingdom of God and having eternal life, he will then stand back and merely watch to see if we will do it. We do not naturally think that if he demands something, he will enable us to do it.

JESUS CAME TO FULFILL THE NEW COVENANT IN HIS BLOOD

But Jesus knew that he had come to fulfill the "new covenant" promised by the prophet Jeremiah. At the end of his life at the Last Supper, he took the cup that represented his blood and said, "This cup that is poured out for you is the *new covenant* in my blood" (Luke 22:20).

What was new about the "new covenant" was

that the commands of God would not merely be written on stone (Exod. 24:12), as in the covenant with Moses, but would now be written on the hearts of God's people. God promised through Jeremiah, "Behold, the days are coming, declares the LORD, when I will make a new covenant with the house of Israel and the house of Judah, not like the covenant that I made with their fathers on the day when I took them by the hand to bring them out of the land of Egypt. . . . But this is the covenant that I will make with the house of Israel after those days, declares the LORD: *I will put my law within them, and I will write it on their hearts*" (Jer. 31:31-33).

Jesus came to inaugurate this new covenant through his life and death and resurrection and by the sending of the Holy Spirit. The prophet Ezekiel wrote that the way the new covenant would secure the obedience of God's people (the striving to enter through the narrow door) was by God's Spirit being given to them and by their own spirit being made new. God said through Ezekiel, "I will put my Spirit within you, and cause you to walk in my statutes. . . . A new spirit I will put within them. I will remove the heart of stone from their flesh and give them a heart

of flesh, that they may walk in my statutes and keep
my rules and obey them" (Ezek. 36:27; 11:19-20).
God's intention was to give his commands *and* the
ability to do them. That is the new covenant.

By his shed blood Jesus purchased this new
covenant for all who trust him. Then, on the basis of
the forgiveness of sins that he obtained for his people
(Matt. 26:28), he gave them the promise of the Holy
Spirit. He said:

> I will ask the Father, and he will give you another
> Helper, to be with you forever, even the Spirit of
> truth . . . he dwells with you and will be in
> you. . . . When the Helper comes, whom I will send
> to you from the Father, the Spirit of truth, who
> proceeds from the Father, he will bear witness about
> me. . . . He will glorify me, for he will take what
> is mine and declare it to you. (John 14:16; 15:26;
> 16:14)

WITHOUT CHRIST OUR STRIVING
WOULD BE LOSING

Therefore, by his death and by the sending of the
Spirit, Jesus obtains the new-covenant promises for
those who trust him. And the heart of that covenant

is that our sins are forgiven and the Spirit of God is given to help us do what Jesus demands, namely, strive to enter by the narrow door. In other words, Jesus' demand that we "strive to enter" does not mean he stands aloof and watches. As Martin Luther wrote in his famous hymn:

> Did we in our own strength confide,
> our striving would be losing;
> Were not the right Man on our side,
> the Man of God's own choosing:
> Dost ask who that may be?
> Christ Jesus, it is He; Lord Sabaoth,
> His Name, from age to age the same,
> and He must win the battle.[1]

We are not left to ourselves in our striving. The command to strive is the command to experience the powerful striving of God on our behalf in fulfillment of his new-covenant promise to cause us to walk in his statutes (Ezek. 36:27). We will see this all the more clearly and forcefully in the next chapter, which deals with the presence of the kingdom of God and the presence of eternal life and the way to maintain hope and joy and peace as we strive to enter through the narrow door.

Truly, I say to you, whoever does not receive the kingdom of God like a child shall not enter it.

MARK 10:15

CHAPTER SIX

OUR JOY IN JESUS SUSTAINS OUR STRIVING

The demand to strive to enter the kingdom of God through the narrow door should be heard in connection with the truth that God has already done something to make that striving full of hope and confidence. We strive not with fretting that we will not enter, but with assurance that not only *will* we enter, but in a decisive sense we have already entered. This may sound paradoxical: Strive to enter, for you have entered. But it is profoundly true for all who trust in Jesus.

THE SECRET OF THE KINGDOM OF GOD: IT IS HERE

At the center of Jesus' message is the claim that both the kingdom of God and eternal life are *present* experiences as well as *future* promises. In other words, when Jesus demands that we strive to enter the kingdom through the narrow door, he is focusing on the future experience of final joy and perfect fellowship with God when the kingdom comes in fullest measure in the future. Strive to enter that.

But the "secret of the kingdom" (Mark 4:11)
that Jesus revealed to his disciples was that the
kingdom had *already* arrived in his ministry and that
his followers enter it *now* and experience its power
even before its final consummation.[1] For example,
Jesus said, "If it is by the finger of God that I cast
out demons, then *the kingdom of God has come upon
you . . .* behold, the kingdom of God *is in the midst
of you*" (Luke 11:20; 17:21). In his ministry the
kingdom of God, which will be consummated in the
future, has come near, and its power is in delivering
people from bondage to Satan and sin.

Which means, for the followers of Jesus, that our
striving to "enter through the narrow door" is done
in the power of the kingdom that we have received
as a free gift. Recall how Jesus put it: "Truly, I say to
you, whoever does not *receive* the kingdom of God
like a child shall not *enter* it" (Mark 10:15). We now
receive it as a gift by faith and experience its power.
By this power of the kingdom we will walk the "hard
way" and enter the "narrow door." Paradoxically,
we strive to *enter* the kingdom from *inside* the
kingdom. The present power of the kingdom is here,

and we have entered into that power by faith. The consummation of the kingdom, with its victory over death and disease and all sin, is still future, and we are not yet there.

ETERNAL LIFE IS OURS NOW

The same interconnection between the future and the present is true of *eternal life*, not just the kingdom of God. On the one hand, Jesus speaks of eternal life as a future inheritance: "Everyone who has left houses or brothers or sisters or father or mother or children or lands, for my name's sake, will receive a hundredfold and *will inherit eternal life*" (Matt. 19:29; cf. 25:46). But on the other hand, he teaches that believing on him means having eternal life now: "Truly, truly, I say to you, whoever hears my word and believes him who sent me has eternal life. He does not come into judgment, but *has passed from death to life*" (John 5:24; cf. 3:36). By trusting Jesus we have eternal life now, but we will come into the fullest experience of it in the future.

THE PRESENCE OF LIFE AND KINGDOM DOES
NOT PRODUCE PRESUMPTION BUT JOY

Jesus' teaching about this truth—that entering the
kingdom of God and entering eternal life are both
present experience and future hope—does not
express itself in presumption and carelessness. It
does not produce the attitude that says, "I'm already
saved; it does not matter how I live. I do not need to
be vigilant. I do not need to strive to enter through
the narrow door." That is not the way a person talks
who has entered eternal life and has been grasped
by the power of God's kingdom. Instead, this truth
expresses itself in joyful striving.

To some people striving does not sound like a
joyful way to live. It sounds burdensome. But that
is not the way followers of Jesus experience it. Of
course, taking up our cross and denying ourselves
and becoming the "slave of all" (Mark 10:44) is
often painful. But it is not oppressive. There is joy
at every turn. This is why Jesus said, "Rejoice . . .
and leap for joy" (Luke 6:23). In fact, it is the joy of
having eternal life now and being in the kingdom of
God now and knowing our sins forgiven now and
enjoying the fellowship of Jesus now that sustains

our ability to strive toward that future entrance through the narrow door into the consummation of God's kingdom. That is the point of the little parable in Matthew 13:44: "The kingdom of heaven is like treasure hidden in a field, which a man found and covered up. Then in his joy he goes and sells all that he has and buys that field." Joy is the sustaining motive for selling all—for striving to enter through the narrow door.

This is an illustration of how doing something difficult and seemingly oppressive—selling all you have—is carried by joy. "*In his joy* he goes and sells all that he has." That is the banner flying over all our striving as we follow Jesus: *In our joy* we fight off every temptation that would destroy our soul with deceptive pleasures or deceptive pain. We fight as those who *must* fight and *will* win. The striving is essential, and its outcome for Christ's sheep is certain. "My sheep hear my voice, and I know them, and they follow me. I give them eternal life, and they will never perish, and no one will snatch them out of my hand" (John 10:27-28).

HELP FOR THE FAINTHEARTED

The demand of Jesus that we "strive to enter through the narrow door" is overarching. It gives a sense of urgency to all his demands. It does not refer to a class of commandments but to all of them. It is a demand that we take all his word seriously. It calls for lifelong, everyday, hour-by-hour vigilance over our thoughts and feelings and actions. Therefore, it troubles some followers of Jesus who are fainthearted. I have tried to help us all take heart. It may be practically useful to close this chapter with a summary list of ways to maintain hope and joy as we strive together to enter through the narrow door.

THE FIGHT IS TO CHERISH WHAT WE HAVE, NOT TO EARN WHAT WE DON'T

First, remember that the main battle is the battle to keep seeing Jesus as the supreme treasure of your life. He does not call us to fight for plastic jewels. Following Jesus is the result of finding a treasure hidden in a field—an infinitely valuable treasure. Then in our joy we gladly "let goods and kindred go, this mortal life also"[2] to enjoy that treasure to the full. Striving to enter through the narrow door is only as hard as treasuring Jesus above all things. The battle is not to do what we don't want, but to want what is infinitely worthy of wanting. The fight is not the oppressive struggle to earn God's final rest, but the satisfying struggle to rest in the peace that Jesus freely gives. "Come to me, all who labor and are heavy laden, and I will give you rest. Take my yoke upon you, and learn from me, for I am gentle and lowly in heart, and you will find rest for your souls. For my yoke is easy, and my burden is light" (Matt. 11:28-30). The demands of Jesus are only as hard to obey as his promises are hard to cherish and his presence is hard to treasure.

JESUS PROMISES TO HELP US DO THE IMPOSSIBLE
Second, remember that Jesus promises to help us obey his demand. "I am the vine; you are the branches. Whoever abides in me and I in him, he it is that bears much fruit, for apart from me you can do nothing" (John 15:5). He promised to be with us to the end of the age (Matt. 28:20). He promised not to leave us like orphans when he returned to heaven, but to come to us and help us (John 14:16-18). He acknowledges that what he demands is impossible,

but then promises omnipotent help: "With man it is impossible, but not with God. For all things are possible with God" (Mark 10:27). Don't think of striving to get his favor. Think of striving with the favor of his help.

FORGIVENESS AND JUSTIFICATION ARE AT THE BOTTOM OF OUR STRIVING

Third, remember that forgiveness of sins and justification by faith are at the bottom of our striving. We do not strive for them. We strive because we have them. Jesus offers forgiveness in Matthew 26:28 ("This is my blood of the covenant, which is poured out for many for the forgiveness of sins"), and he offers justification in Luke 18:13-14 ("The tax collector, standing far off, would not even lift up his eyes to heaven, but beat his breast, saying, 'God, be merciful to me, a sinner!' I tell you, this man went down to his house justified"). Our standing with God as forgiven and righteous is the ground of our striving, not the goal of our striving. We must strive to enter because that is the mark of the one who belongs to Christ. If we do not strive, we do not bear the mark of belonging to Jesus. But the striving does not create the relationship. The secure relationship produces the joyful striving.

Perfection Awaits the Age to Come

Fourth, keep in mind that perfection awaits the age to come. We do wish that we could be free from all sinful feelings and thoughts and actions now. That longing and that labor is part of our striving. But we would despair if perfection in this life were a prerequisite for entering through the narrow door. There is a perfection required ("If you would be perfect, go, sell what you possess," Matt. 19:21), but no human can achieve it. Only Jesus fulfills all righteousness (Matt. 3:15). This is why he teaches us to pray, not once, but every day, "Forgive us our debts" (Matt. 6:12). Very bluntly Jesus calls his disciples (not would-be disciples, but committed disciples) "evil"—"If you then, *who are evil*, know how to give good gifts to your children . . ." (Matt. 7:11). Let us then take heart that the mark of a true follower of Jesus is not yet perfection but rather unrelenting battle against sin. We fail, but we do not fall away.[3] We stumble, but we do not fall headlong into apostasy.

JESUS PRAYS FOR US THAT WE NOT FAIL

Fifth, remember that the reason we do not fall away
is that Jesus is not only helping us by his presence
and Spirit, but is also praying for us. Jesus said to
Peter, who was about to deny him three times, "I
have prayed for you that your faith may not fail.
And when you have turned again, strengthen your
brothers" (Luke 22:32). Jesus knew Peter would
sin, and he knew he would turn back from his sinful
denial. He said, "*When* you have turned," not "*If* you
turn." He did not use his sovereign power to prevent
Peter's sin, but he did use it to prevent Peter's falling
away. There is no reason to think Jesus has stopped
praying like that for his loved ones. God will answer
his Son when he prays, "Holy Father, keep them in
your name, which you have given me, that they may
be one, even as we are one" (John 17:11).

WE ARE STRIVING TO ENTER OUR FATHER'S HOUSE

Sixth, remember your position as a true *child* of God.
Jesus taught his disciples to know and trust God as
their personal *Father* in heaven. Before Jesus came,
Israel as a people thought of God as the Father of
the nation, but relating to God *individually* as Father

was unusual. But Jesus made it central and referred to it again and again. The implication was: God loves you personally as his child and will take care of you. Bank on it.

This did not apply to everyone. For example, he said to some, "If God were your Father, you would love me, for I came from God and I am here. . . . You are of your father the devil, and your will is to do your father's desires" (John 8:42, 44). This is very important for Jesus' followers: If God is our Father, we love Jesus. This means that being a child of God involves having a new nature. The mark of this new nature is a love for Jesus. Therefore, loving Jesus is a sure sign that we are the children of God.

And if we are already children, we may have deep confidence that our striving to enter the narrow door of our Father's house will succeed. He will see to it. He is our Father now. He is not watching to see if we will strive hard enough to become his children. He is actively helping us get home. For example, when we are tested publicly to see if we will testify of Jesus as we ought, Jesus says not to worry: "It is not you who speak, but the Spirit of *your Father* speaking through you" (Matt. 10:20). Not a single

sparrow falls to the ground apart from "your Father,"
Jesus says. "Fear not, therefore; you are of more
value than many sparrows" (Matt. 10:29, 31). That's
the spirit of confidence that comes from being a child
of God.

YOUR NAME IS WRITTEN IN HEAVEN

Seventh, remember, as you strive to enter through
the narrow door, that your name is written in heaven.
Jesus said, "Do not rejoice in this, that the spirits are
subject to you, but rejoice that your names are written
in heaven" (Luke 10:20). If everybody's name is
written in heaven, there is no reason to rejoice, but
many are on the way to destruction, not the narrow
door: "The way is easy that leads to destruction, and
those who enter by it are many" (Matt. 7:13). Not all
names are written there. Having your name written
in heaven means that God will deliver you from evil
and bring you to his kingdom. Jesus had read about
this book in a prophet he knew well, Daniel 12:1:
"There shall be a time of trouble, such as never has
been since there was a nation till that time. But at that
time your people shall be delivered, *everyone whose
name shall be found written in the book.*"

You Were Chosen by God and Given to Jesus

Eighth, remember that Jesus is not collecting disciples whom God has not known. God knew his own first and wrote them in his book. Now the Father is drawing them to his Son for salvation. "All that the Father gives me will come to me, and whoever comes to me I will never cast out" (John 6:37). The followers of Jesus belonged to God first and then were given to Jesus (John 17:9). If someone comes to Jesus, it is because the Father knew him and gave him to the Son. That's why Jesus said, "No one can come to me unless it is granted him by the Father" (John 6:65). When they come, Jesus reveals the Father to them, and the Father keeps them from falling away: "I have manifested your name to the people whom you gave me out of the world. Yours they were, and you gave them to me" (John 17:6). "My Father, who has given them to me, is greater than all, and no one is able to snatch them out of the Father's hand" (John 10:29). When you remember and rejoice that you are a chosen child of God, your striving will not be oppressive or slavish.

JESUS SUSTAINS OUR STRIVING BY HIS JOY

Ninth, remember that joy in God is the key way that Jesus enables us to strive to enter through the narrow door. First, Jesus says, "I am the vine; you are the branches . . . apart from me you can do nothing" (John 15:5). Then he says, "These things I have spoken to you, that my joy may be in you, and that your joy may be full" (John 15:11). In other words, the way Jesus enables us to strive successfully to enter through the narrow door is by imparting to us his joy. Then later he adds, "No one will take your joy from you" (John 16:22). This joy in Jesus and all that God is for us in him sustains lifelong striving to enter though the narrow door.

OUR STRIVING WILL NOT BE IN VAIN

Vigilance is the mark of the followers of Jesus. They know that "the gate is wide and the way is easy that leads to destruction" (Matt. 7:13). They are serious about life. Heaven and hell are at stake. Therefore, they are seriously joyful. The Son of God has rescued them from the guilt and power of sin. They are children of God. Their names are written in heaven. They have received the Helper, the Spirit of truth. They have the promise of Jesus to be with them to the end of the age. They know that he is praying for them. They rejoice that they stand righteous before God because of Jesus. They have received the kingdom. They have eternal life as a present possession. And they marvel that no one can snatch them out of God's hand. In this joy they are energized to strive to enter by the narrow door. And they are confident their striving will not be in vain.

NOTES

CHAPTER TWO

1. For more on what obedience to Jesus looks like in the secular workplace, see the chapter "Making Much of Christ from 8 to 5" in John Piper, *Don't Waste Your Life* (Wheaton, Ill.:Crossway Books, 2003), 131-154.

CHAPTER THREE

1. I wrote a little book to get people started on this path, *The Dangerous Duty of Delight* (Sisters, Ore.: Multnomah, 2001), and a bigger book to go deeper, *Desiring God: Meditations of a Christian Hedonist* (Sisters, Ore.: Multnomah, 2003).

2. C. S. Lewis, *The Weight of Glory, and Other Addresses* (Grand Rapids, Mich.: Eerdmans, 1965), 2.

3. Ibid., 1.

4. Jonathan Edwards, "The Pleasantness of Religion," in *The Sermons of Jonathan Edwards: A Reader*, ed. Wilson H. Kimnach, Kenneth P. Minkema, and Douglas A. Sweeney (New Haven, Conn.: Yale University Press, 1999), 23-24.

5. Ibid. The preceding and following paragraphs are adapted from John Piper, "A God-Entranced Vision of All Things: Why We Need Jonathan Edwards 300 Years Later," in *A God-Entranced Vision of All Things: The Legacy of Jonathan Edwards*, ed. John Piper and Justin Taylor (Wheaton, Ill.: Crossway Books, 2004), 29.

6. The word "complete" (*peplērōntai*) translates the same Greek word (*plēroō*) that is used in John 15:11 (*plērōthē*), 16:24 (*peplērōmenē*), and 17:13 (*peplērōmenēn*). Each refers to the joy of the disciples being full. Since John 3:29 and 16:24 base that joy on the presence of Jesus, we may assume the other two very likely refer to that as well.

7. Quoted from an unpublished sermon, "Sacrament Sermon on Canticles 5:1" (circa 1729).

CHAPTER FOUR

1. Even though he pronounces a woe on the rich (Luke 6:24) and pronounces blessedness on the poor (Luke 6:20), he does not mean that mere finances make one blessed or damnable. We know this, first, because he also says, "Woe to you who laugh now" (Luke 6:25) and "Blessed are you who weep now" (Luke 6:21), and we know from this very context that disciples are to rejoice now (Luke 6:23). So Jesus assumes that we are going to qualify his seemingly absolute statements here. The rich and the poor who are blessed are those for whom Jesus is their supreme treasure and therefore seek to use their wealth or poverty to magnify the worth of Jesus above money and what it can buy. We also know Jesus did not pronounce damnation and blessedness on mere financial condition because he told the rich young ruler to sell all that he had (Mark 10:21) but commended Zacchaeus for giving half of his money away (Luke 19:8-9). However, having said all that, it is significant that Jesus considers wealth so dangerous and poverty so auspicious; he simply says woe to the one and blessed be the other.

CHAPTER FIVE

1. Martin Luther, "A Mighty Fortress Is Our God."

CHAPTER SIX

1. "The mystery of the Kingdom is the coming of the Kingdom into history in advance of its apocalyptic manifestation. It is, in short, 'fulfillment without consummation.' . . . The new truth, now given by revelation in the person and mission of Jesus, is that the Kingdom which is to come finally in apocalyptic power, as foreseen in Daniel, has in fact entered into the world in advance in a hidden form to work secretly within and among men." George Ladd, *The Presence of the Future* (Grand Rapids, Mich.: Eerdmans, 1974), 222.

2. Martin Luther, "A Mighty Fortress Is Our God."

3. The term "fall away" can refer to a temporary departure from Christ in fear followed by repentance and restoration. For example, in Matthew 26:31, Jesus said to his disciples, "You will all fall away because of me this night. For it is written, 'I will strike the shepherd, and the sheep of the flock will be scattered.'" But I am using the term here in its more absolute sense. True followers of Jesus will not fall away utterly and finally.

Recommended Reading
from John Piper

What Jesus Demands from the World
The Passion of Jesus Christ
Seeing and Savoring Jesus Christ
Fifty Reasons Why Jesus Came to Die
Don't Waste Your Life
Desiring God
When I Don't Desire God
Taste and See
God Is the Gospel
Future Grace

For a complete list of available titles, please visit www.desiringGod.org.

Crossway Books, a ministry of Good News Publishers, graciously allowed the use, in this booklet, of selections from *What Jesus Demands from the World* by John Piper. Please visit them at www.crossway.com.

Recommendations

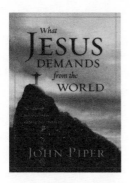

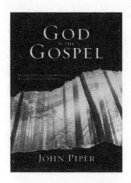

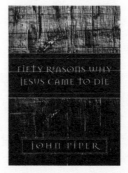

❖ desiringGod

Desiring God exists to spread a passion for the supremacy of God in all things for the joy of all peoples through Jesus Christ. We exist for your joy, because God is most glorified in us when we are most satisfied in him. Please visit our website for hundreds of free and discounted God-centered resources from Pastor John Piper. These resources include books, CDs, DVDs, sermons, articles, children's Sunday school curricula, and more.

Desiring God
2601 East Franklin Avenue
Minneapolis, MN 55406-1103
Toll Free: 1.888.346.4700
Web: www.desiringGod.org

www.desiringGod.org

On our website you will find hundreds of resources and products to help you find your joy in God. In our resource library you will find hundreds of sermons, articles, online books, biographies, seminars, and other resources to read, listen, and watch—all without charge. In our store you will find all of John Piper's books and many CD albums, MP3s, and DVDs of his messages available for purchase.

Whatever-You-Can-Afford

Desiring God does not exist to make money. We exist to spread the gospel. This is why we offer our online resources for free and sell our other resources for as little as possible. Even though we keep our prices low, we realize that sometimes individuals simply cannot afford to pay. For these friends, we have a Whatever-You-Can-Afford policy. We will accept whatever people are able to pay—even if it's nothing. It makes us very happy to give freely what has been freely given to us (Matthew 10:8). And we never want to make cost "an obstacle in the way of the gospel of Christ" (1 Corinthians 9:12). So if you would like a copy of a book or audio resource we offer, but your limited cash-flow prevents it, don't be ashamed! Just contact us and let us know what you would like, and it will be our pleasure to fill your request.

The Author

John Piper is the Pastor for Preaching and Vision at Bethlehem Baptist Church in Minneapolis, Minnesota. He grew up in Greenville, South Carolina, and studied at Wheaton College, where he first sensed God's call to enter the ministry. He went on to earn degrees from Fuller Theological Seminary (B.D.) and the University of Munich (D. Theol.). For six years he taught Biblical Studies at Bethel College in St. Paul, Minnesota, and in 1980 accepted the call to serve as pastor at Bethlehem. He is the author of numerous books and his preaching is featured on the daily radio program Desiring God. He and his wife Noël have four sons, one daughter, and an increasing number of grandchildren.